Greetings from Burlington, Vermont

Mary L. Martin &
Dinah Roseberry

Schiffer Publishing Ltd®
4880 Lower Valley Road Atglen, Pennsylvania 19310

Published by Schiffer Publishing Ltd.
4880 Lower Valley Road
Atglen, PA 19310
Phone: (610) 593-1777; Fax: (610) 593-2002
E-mail: Info@schifferbooks.com

Library of Congress Control Number: 2007920181

Designed by Mark David Bowyer
Type set in ZapfChancery Bd BT / Korrina BT

ISBN: 978-0-7643-2632-5
Printed in China

In Europe, Schiffer books are distributed by
Bushwood Books
6 Marksbury Ave.
Kew Gardens
Surrey TW9 4JF England
Phone: 44 (0) 20 8392-8585; Fax: 44 (0) 20 8392-9876
E-mail: info@bushwoodbooks.co.uk
Website: www.bushwoodbooks.co.uk
Free postage in the U.K., Europe; air mail at cost.

Contents

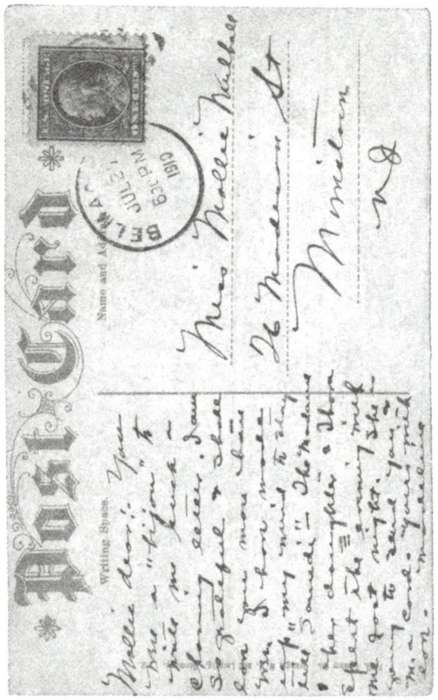

An Introduction to Burlington, Vermont

You may find it difficult to find a more beautiful place in the world than scenic Burlington, Vermont. From land to lake and from work to play, Burlington fills the bill for just the right place to be—past, present, or future. Visual wonders abounded in earlier times, displayed here through precious views of days past—times when coastal areas provided bays, beaches, and boats; and land excursions offered life in lovely park-like and wilderness settings.

Historically rich and visually alive, this coastal city has been called Vermont's West Coast. With Lake Champlain, one of the nation's largest and most beautiful lakes, and the Adirondack Mountains towering with majestic splendor, visitors and residents are never far from any particular brand of paradise.

Be prepared to be immersed in nostalgic marvel with over 240 vintage, hand-tinted, photographic, and sepia-toned postcards that span from the late 1800s through the 1940s, paying homage to this romantic city by the lake. Whether it's the excitement of Burlington's turn-of-the-century city streets and architectural excellence, the busy college life, or historic and natural wonders, enjoy a time that carries yesterday into today. Burlington will delight you as you take time to remember her as she once was.

Historic Images Through Postcards

Postcards are said to be the most popular collectible history has ever known. The urge to horde them sprang up with the birth of this means of communication at the turn of the twentieth century, and has endured great changes in the printing industry. Today, postcard shows take place every weekend somewhere in the country, or the world, and millions of pieces of ephemera lie in wait for those who collect obscure topics or town views.

Postcards once served as the email of their day. They were the fastest, most popular means of communication, beginning in the 1890s in the United States. These timely cards provided a way to send visual scenes through the mail along with brief messages– a way to enchant friends and family with the places travelers visited, to send local scenes, or to share favorite topics of imagery. They even provided the latest breaking news, as images of fires, floods, shipwrecks, and festivals were often available in postcard form within hours of an event. Moreover, mail was delivered to most urban homes in the United States at least twice a day. So someone might send a morning postcard inviting a friend to dinner that evening, and receive an RSVP in time to shop for food.

The messages shared and the beautiful scenes combine to create the timeless appeal of postcards as a collectible. Most importantly, history is recorded by the pictures of the times, moments in time reflecting an alluring past.

Dating Historic Postcards

Pioneer Era (1893-1898): Most pioneer cards in today's collections begin with cards placed on sale at the Columbian Exposition in Chicago on May 1, 1893. These were illustrations on government printed postal cards and privately printed souvenir cards. The government cards had the printed one-cent stamp, while souvenir cards required a two-cent adhesive postage stamp to be applied. Writing was not permitted on the address side of the card.

Private Mailing Card Era (1898-1901): On May 19, 1898, private printers were granted permission, by an act of Congress, to print and sell cards that bore the inscription "Private Mailing Card." A one-cent adhesive stamp was required. A dozen or more American printers began to take postcards seriously. Writing was still not permitted on the back.

Post Card Era - Undivided Back (1901-1907): New U.S. postal regulations on December 24, 1901 stipulated that the words "Post Card" should be printed at the top of the address side of privately printed cards.

Government-issued cards were to be designated as "Postal Cards." Writing was still not permitted on the address side. In this era, private citizens began to take black and white photographs and have them printed on paper with post card backs.

Early Divided Back Era (1907-1914): Postcards with a divided back were permitted in Britain in 1902, but not in the U.S. until March 1, 1907. The address was to be written on the right side; the left side was for writing messages. Many millions of cards were published in this era. Up to this point, most postcards were printed in Germany, which was far ahead of the United States in the use of lithographic processes. With the advent of World War I, the supply of postcards for American consumption switched from Germany to England and the United States.

White Border Era (1915-1930): Most United States postcards were printed during this period. To save ink, publishers left a clear border around the view, thus these postcards are referred to as "White Border" cards. The relatively high cost of labor, along with inexperience and changes in public taste, resulted in the production of poor quality cards during this period. Furthermore, strong competition in a narrowing market caused many publishers to go out of business.

Linen Era (1930-1944): New printing processes allowed printing on postcards with high rag content that created a textured finish. These cheap cards allowed the use of gaudy dyes for coloring.

Photochrome Era (1945 to date): "Chrome" postcards began to dominate the scene soon after the Union Oil Company placed them in its western service stations in 1939. Mike Roberts pioneered with his "WESCO" cards soon after World War II. Three-dimensional postcards also appeared in this era.

Example of a postcard with an undivided back. Senders could only write the address on this side of the card. Any message needed to be written on the front of the card along with the picture.

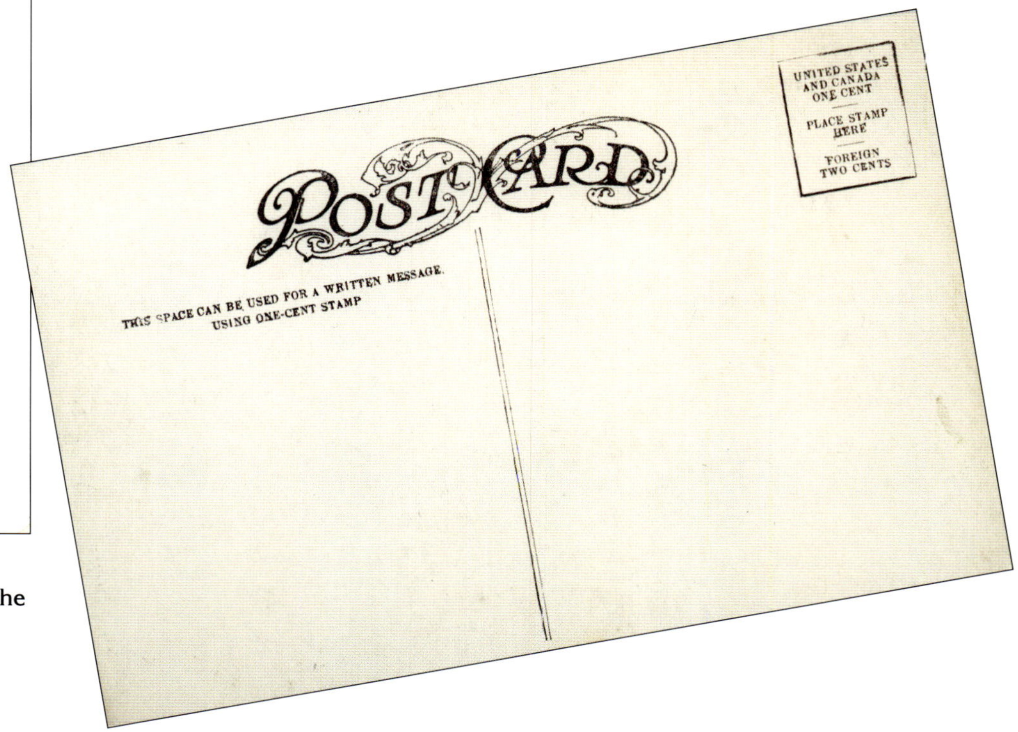

Sample of a postcard with a divided back. Senders were allowed to put an address on the right hand side of the postcard and a message on the left side.

A Brief Historical Overview

Burlington is the largest city in the state of Vermont, and also the County Seat (Shire town—as termed by parts of New England and Canada) for Chittenden County. There is somewhat of a mystery around the naming of this scenic port town that has historians choosing between two possible occurrences. The first thought is that Burlington was named after the Earl of Burlington—though because there are several Earls that could feasibly be the namesake, no one knows which Earl might hold the historic honor.

The second possibility has been said to be a more popular and plausible occurrence. Records indicate that the Burling family had a prominence in Vermont in the 1700s and are listed as being grantees of eleven other towns in the area. Ten of those towns were recorded at the grant office during the same day. It has been suggested that on this "busiest day in the grant office's history," a property clerk mixed up the paperwork for two different towns making the city we see today Burlington, rather than another name (probably Colchester).

Burlington was chartered in 1763, but it was not until the 1770s that settlers came, after a fort at the Winooski Falls was built by Ethan and Ira Allen. In fact, it was not until after the Revolutionary War that settlers seriously began clearing land for farming. Ethan Allen built his home in Burlington in 1787, near the Winooski River, and it remains at the same location today. Ira Allen donated land for the University of Vermont in 1791 to build an agricultural educational facility, further promoting the use of Burlington's land to develop individuals in efforts of farming and agriculture.

As Vermont's first incorporated city, the northwestern section of the town became the City of Burlington in 1864, while the more rural south of the city became the new town of South Burlington.

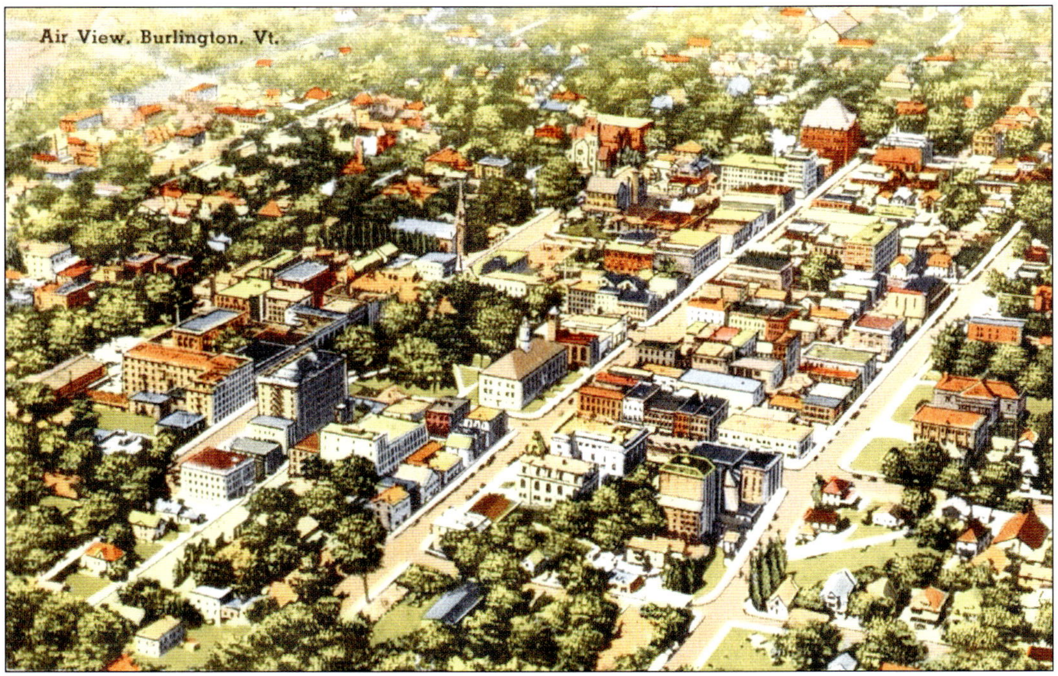

An bird's eye view of Burlington.

Circa 1930s, $3-5

The most historic body of water in North America, Lake Champlain provides trade, recreation, and relaxation for all who visit.

Circa 1907, $1-3

The Ethan Allen Tower was built to honor the revolutionary war hero, Ethan Allen. It is located at the Ethan Allen Park on North Avenue in Burlington.

Cancelled 1911 , $1-3

The hustle and bustle of Burlington as the city streets come alive with traffic. Note the Unitarian Church at the base of the street and F. W. Woolworths to the left.

Cancelled 1941, $6-8

A college town, the grounds of the University of Vermont are beautifully landscaped making attending this facility a joy to students.

Circa 1907, $3-5

Buildings

Burlington's impressive architecture and heritage is preserved through a selection of buildings, ranging from views of historic majesty to artistic magnificence in the following pages. From the community-inspired YMCA to the exquisite elegance of the Grass Mount, once the home of Governor Van Ness, the buildings of Burlington provide a precious view into a time passed.

The expertly designed landscape at the Ethan Allen Club in Burlington.

Circa 1907, $3-5

The history of Oakledge Manor begins in 1793—in a much smaller home than shown here—when the Webb family (also affiliated with Shelburne Farms) built their residence on two Burlington lots.

Circa 1900s, $4-6

After many sales and managers of the land over the years, the property was named Oakledge Manor in 1929 and became a summer resort. By 1934, Oakledge covered 225 acres.

Circa 1900s, $3-5

Plagued over the years by fire, business agreements and changes, and eventually demolition, today there is no trace of the Oakledge Manor left in what is now called the beautiful Oakledge Park and Beach.

Circa 1900s, $2-4

Grass Mount, now used as a dormitory for the University of Vermont, was once the residence of Governor Cornelius P. Van Ness.

Circa 1907, $3-5

The YMCA of Burlington was founded in 1866 and was initially a men's prayer group, holding meetings above a storefront on College Street. As Burlington thrived, the "Y" grew into an organization that could provide board, physical education, and cultural programs to the young men of the city. In the early 1900s, services were extended to women and children, and by the end of the century, the "Y" was the largest provider of child care programs in Vermont.

Circa 1930s, $3-5

The Hegemeer for Tourists. The current owners, who conduct Bible discussions with area students, advise that the house is a copy of a Sears kitset house, and that many others like it were built in the area. The original workshop is still in the corner of the basement.

Circa 1907, $4-6

The Robert Hull Fleming Museum at the University of Vermont was opened in 1931 and was thought to be "a practical place of learning — a vibrant, ongoing educational institution for both children and adults."

Circa 1907, $4-6

Constructed initially as the Providence Orphan Asylum by the diocese of Burlington, the asylum was run by the Sisters of Providence from Montreal. An influx of orphans, sisters, and elderly led to an addition to the building for classrooms, dormitories, and a gymnasium in 1941. Some time later, it became known as St. Joseph's, and it was found that more and more children placed here were from broken homes. By 1960, there was no longer a need for a facility of this size because other organizations were being initiated to care for these children.

Circa 1914, $4-6

The Home for Destitute Children on 447 Main Street opened in 1865, surviving overwhelming challenges over the years to assist the multitudes of children requiring services. In 1945, the Home was renamed, The Children's Home, showing a change from orphanage status to an institution prepared to help children in a treatment-oriented fashion. Today, the Baird Center takes the place of the home with a new facility built at the location.

Circa 1907, $4-6

The H. W. Allen and Company in Burlington is a large dry goods establishment. In 1910, H. W. Allen's interests in the company were bought by Frank Abernethy.

Circa early 1900s, $5-7

The Twist O'Hill Lodge, located on Route 2 is the forefront for Mount Mansfield. In 1968, the lodge became the main building for the Pine Ridge School for teenagers with learning disabilities.

Circa 1907, $4-6

Churches

Religious practices were as important in Burlington as they were in all the major cities of the United States throughout history. Growing spiritual needs closely recognized in Burlington provided for many varied religions and places to worship, including the faiths of Catholic, Episcopal, Unitarian, Methodist, and others. Though social and natural calamities sometimes plagued the spiritual structures shown here, faith was maintained, and progressed to the welcoming community worship sites known today.

Saint Mark's Church is still offering full services to the community from its parish at 1251 North Avenue.

Cancelled 1951 , $3-5

St. Paul's Episcopal Church was not slated to see plans for the building of a new cathedral to replace the one you see here until 1971. The City made plans to build a downtown mall on the land where St. Paul's had stood.

Cancelled 1909, $4-6

St. Joseph's Church. This Roman Catholic Church was built circa 1890 to provide services for Burlington's French Canadian immigrant population. Though it was originally located on Archibald Street, growth called for the construction of the new church on Allen Street in 1883.

Cancelled 1907, $4-6

The St. Paul's Church was built in 1833. In 1910, there was a fire (and another fire again in 1971)—burning the church to the ground as the result of arson. (Oddly enough, the next year, a Roman Catholic Cathedral, a block away, was also destroyed by an arsonist's fire.)

Circa 1930s, $3-5

Another St. Paul's Episcopal Church view before the fire. The City traded a larger parcel of land a short distance away, overlooking Lake Champlain and the Adirondacks for the new location of the present St. Paul's Cathedral.

Circa 1907, $4-6

A view of the St. Paul's Rectory and Parish House.

Circa 1907, $4-6

Mount St. Mary Academy was home at one time to as many as one hundred Sisters of Mercy. The Burlington chapter was formed in 1874. The Mount St. Mary Academy opened in 1886 with all of the Sisters of Mercy relocating here by 1888.

Circa 1914, $4-6

In 1925, the Academy was expanded, and Trinity College held its first classes in the expanded area. For eighty-one years, the Academy served as a Catholic high school and college preparatory education facility for girls. The Academy closed in 1967.

Cancelled 1907, $5-7

St. Mary's Cathedral in Burlington. This cathedral was initially to be used as a parish church, but became a cathedral church when the Fall River Diocese was created in 1904.

Circa 1907, $4-6

Another view of Mary's Cathedral. In August of 1852, the cornerstone of the Cathedral was laid. There was already a small wooden church standing on the site, but it was too small to serve the population.

Circa early 1900s, $4-6

The College Street Congregational Church of Burlington. In 1863, construction of the church commenced and services were held in a basement chapel in 1865. Programs for Civil War orphans, unwed mothers, elderly women, and feeding the needy were all part of the church's community involvement.

Circa 1914, $4-6

The First Congregational Church in Burlington was part of the merger talks between the College Street Congregational Church and the Unitarian Church in 1931. A vote was taken at a joint meeting with the Unitarian Society in the merger discussions of 1931 that resulted in a tie. The College Street Congretional church withdrew from further discussions.

Cancelled 1912, $4-6

In 1816, The Unitarian Church, Burlington, Vermont was built by the First Congregational Society.

Circa 1907, $3-5

The Methodist Episcopal Church was founded in 1823 by the signing of the Articles of Association of the church by fifteen believers. Plans for the church building began in 1831 and the building was completed in 1832. But even then, the congregation became too large for the building. The present church was built and dedicated in 1870.

Circa 1907, $4-6

The Episcopal Institute at Rock Point has been a location of the Summer College of Languages since 1884 during summer vacation. Students attending have been aged from six to sixty.

Cancelled 1915, $3-5

The Episcopal Institute has acted as an annex to college buildings for students with the beautiful landscaping a way to combine study and nature.

Circa 1907, $3-5

A view of the Bishop's House at Rock Point, a wonderful property having the right measure of the wilds and seclusion, with the rewards of nearby culture.

Cancelled 1913, $3-5

Bishop Louis de Goesbriand began to raise funds for this new cathedral in 1860. (Until then, worshipers were served at the Old St. Mary's Church.) In 1867, the Cathedral of Immaculate Conception became the first church in New England designed, created, and dedicated as a Cathedral Church.

Cancelled 1908, $4-6

Another view of The Cathedral of Immaculate Conception. In 1904, a fifteen-foot statue of Mary, Our Lady of Lourdes, sat atop the Cathedral of Immaculate conception. Though the cathedral was destroyed in 1972, the statue atop the Cathedral survived and was kept in storage for nineteen years, then donated to St. Anne's Shrine.

Circa 1930s, $3-5

The cornerstone for the Ira Allen Chapel located at the University of Pennsylvania was laid in 1925 and constructin of the chapel completed the following year. This chapel was built to relieve the crowded chapel conditions on the second floor of the Old Mill (now known as the John Dewey Lounge).

Circa 1930s, $3-5

An inside view of the Ira Allen Chapel. The message on the card relays, "We have chapel in this lovely building every Wednesday."

Cancelled 1941, $3-5

The domed bell tower of the Ira Allen Chapel rises 165 feet above the university campus. This chapel was built to hold 1,000 people.

Cancelled 1941, $3-5

The Masonic Temple in Burlington. The Masons (Freemasons) is a fraternity that is inclusive of all people working toward doing away with division and strife. Their mission is to help all unite and work together for greater good.

Cancelled 1920, $4-6

Lodging

Whether looking at the lovely hand-tinted images of the grand hotels, like the Van Ness and the Vermont, or the photographic wonders of the Cabins at Lake Champlain, Burlington's lodging has always been an experience in quintessential beauty, luxury, and relaxation.

The Van Ness House, as it was sometimes called, had an artesian well 360 feet deep.

Circa 1907, 4-6

The Hotel Van Ness was the only hotel in Burlington with verandas.

Circa 1907, $4-6

The Hotel Burlington. Notice the awnings that shade the sidewalk area in front of the hotel.

Cancelled 1908, $4-6

With a beautiful park atmosphere very nearby and a fine roof garden, complete with grill and promenade on the premises, Hotel Van Ness was considered a luxury accommodation.

Cancelled 1941, $3-5

The East O'Lake Inn, a grand Victorian Inn.

Circa 1907, $4-6

The New Sherwood in Burlington has a lovely rooftop garden with a view of the lake beyond.

Circa 1914, $4-6

Hotels Vermont and Van Ness, two very modern and popular hotels for their time.

Circa 1914, $5-7

Another view of the Hotel Vermont. Three hotels, the Burlington, Van Ness, and Vermont, were all located at the corner of St. Paul Street and Main Street.

Circa 1907, $5-7

The lovely Hyde Park Inn located in the Lamoille Valley on the northern scenic route from Bretton Woods to Burlington. It boasts of an excellent golf course.

Circa 1930s, $3-5

The Allenwood Inn on Lake Champlain. The Inn's dining room and foyer overlook the Lake.

Circa 1930s, $3-5

Inside the Allenwood Inn, the Foyer is decoracted in elegance but with a relaxing aire that shows the charm of the day.

Circa 1930s, $3-5

The Japanese Garden at the Allenwood Inn.

Circa 1930s, $3-5

The Colonial Motor Court at 462 Shelburne Street in Burlington accommodates 50 guests. There are twenty one- and two-room cottages, each with bath—for the discriminating traveler.

Circa 1930s, $3-5

The Ethan Allen Park Cabins at 1024 North Avenue in Burlington are advertised as new and modern—with or without kitchenettes. The cabins are also heated, and have showers with hot and cold water. A private beach and boating is noted as also provided.

Circa 1914, $4-6

Another view of the Champlain Park Cabins, but this postcard boasts of property spanning 106 Lake acres. Though the card advertises Lake Bathing, the message scribbled on the back tells the reader that this particular visitor was glad to have extra blankets during their stay—they did not go bathing in the Lake. This note was made in August of 1946.

Cancelled 1946, $5-7

The Cabins at Champlain Park are located on 55 acres just four miles south of Burlington on the Lake. Each cabin has a hot shower and a flushing toilet.

Circa 1914, $4-6

Education

From grammar school through college, these images from the first half of the twentieth century show the distinct beauty that Burlington offers to students and educators who study and work here from around the world. Known as some of the most lovely (and relevant) educational facilities recognized at the turn-of-the-century, these vintage hand-tinted and sepia-toned postcards will take you back to the early days of education in New England.

Burlington has always been known as a premier college town. The University of Vermont, shown in many of these images, was chartered in 1791 as the fifth college in New England, paving the way for students from all walks of life to receive an education of excellence. Lush landscaping and wondrous mountainous backdrops add to the educational significance of the time.

One of the picturesque grammar schools in the Burlington School District.

Cancelled 1946, $4-6

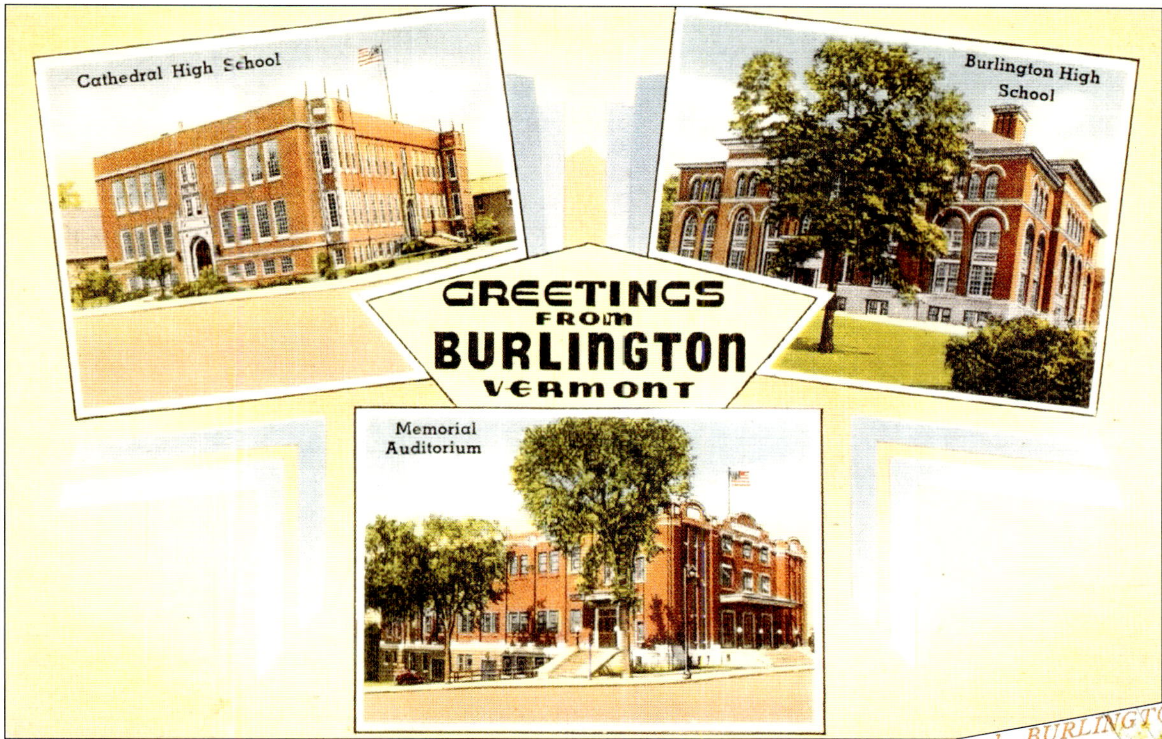

Greetings from three educational facilities of Burlington—Cathedral High School, Burlington High School and Memorial Auditorium! Burlington Academy, established in 1816, was not used solely for high school students until 1829. By 1871, it had relocated to the corner of South Willard and South Union Streets. It was then that a new 46-week school year came to be and the school was renamed Burlington Union High School.

Cancelled 1946, $4-6

Edmunds High School was opened in 1900 at the corner of Main and South Union Streets. The property for the school was sold to the City of Burlington for $15,000 (a small portion of the property value at the time) by the Honorable George Franklin Edmunds, whose family was using the property as a farm.

Cancelled 1907, $5-7

The Edmunds High School is now known at the Edmunds Middle School.

Circa 1907, $4-6

Cathedral High School.

Circa 1930s, $3-5

Trinity College, a premier Roman Catholic college, was founded in 1925 by the Sisters of Mercy to afford educational opportunities for women. Located on twenty acres in the Green Mountains near Lake Champlain, Trinity students were required to take both religion and philosophy in their studies. The facility is now closed, the property purchased by the University of Vermont.

Cancelled 1930, $4-6

St. Michael's College. In 1904, this Catholic educational institution opened with the enrollment of thirty-four students (aged from ten to twenty-two). At that time it was called the Saint Michael's Institute.

Circa 1914, $4-6

An air view of the University of Vermont and Burlington. Chartered in 1791 under the name of University of the Green Mountains, or, as in the Latin Universitas Viridis Montis (VVM), the University of Vermont is the fifth oldest university in New England.

Cancelled 1938, $3-5

The University merged with the State Agricultural College in 1862 (after passing of the Morrill Land-Grant College Act) and the combined name of The University of Vermont and State Agricultural College has been in place ever since.

Cancelled 1917, $3-5

Another view of Campus and College Buildings. Ira Allen (honored as founder) is responsible for much of the initial funding and planning for the University. His statue is located on the University's main green.

Cancelled 1920, $3-5

University of Vermont Row. Burlington residents helped fund the first University building—twice. Fire destroyed it in 1824 and a replacement (Old Mill) was built.

Circa 1907, $4-6

College Row. Throughout the University of Vermont's history, there has been strong commitment to equality and fairness. This was the first American college or university to have a charter stating that "rules, regulations, and by-laws shall not tend to give preference to any religious sect or denomination whatsoever."

Circa 1930s, $3-5

Another picturesque view of College Row.

Circa 1914, $3-5

University Place. University property, over the years, has evolved from open pastures to lush park-like landscaping in today's more informal settings.

Cancelled 1912, $3-5

The first cornerstone for the Old Mill was laid by the Marquis de Lafayette—a French general who became a commander in the American Revolution. The statue of Lafayette stands on University Row.

Circa 1907, $3-5

The bronze life-size state of Lafayette was commissioned by John Purple Howard in 1883.

Cancelled 1909, $3-5

Another view of the University of Vermont.

Circa early 1900s, $4-6

Restone Hall, Girls' Dormitory at the University of Vermont. The University went against prior customs by admitting two women as students in 1871. It was the first University to welcome female students into Phi Beta Kappa—the country's oldest collegiate and academic honor society.

Circa 1914, $4-6

Robinson Hall at University of Vermont. Originally built to serve as a carriage house and stable, the University of Vermont acquired it in 1921 to be used as a women's dormitory. The original building dates back to 1889.

Circa 1914, $4-6

The Converse Dormitory. At the rear of Converse Hall, Mount Mansfield stands providing students with a magnificent view.

Circa 1914, $3-5

The Ira Allen Chapel is no longer used for regular services. Instead, today, special events, ceremonies, and campus meetings are held here.

Circa 1914, $4-6

The Ira Allen Monument. Ira Allen, brother of Ethan Allen, was one of the founders of Vermont and a member of the Vermont Legislature during 1776-1777.

Circa 1907, $3-5

The Waterman Building. Built in 1940-41 as a memorial to his wife, Anna, Senator Charles W. Waterman (class of 1885) gave the Waterman Building to the University as a gift.

Cancelled 1943, $3-5

The Waterman Building was the largest academic building on campus and provided office space, classrooms, and meeting rooms. Initially, there were even several apartments available for faculty and a bowling alley in the basement for recreation. Additionally, the building held a large dining hall and kitchen, as well as library storage space.

Circa 1907, $4-6

Williams Science Hall on University Row was funded by a gift from Edward H. Williams of the Baldwin Locomotive Company in Philadelphia. Built in 1896 with state-of-the-art scientific equipment and facilities, Williams Hall was ahead of its time. It now houses the Art and Anthropology departments.

Circa 1914, $4-6

The Medical College Building. The University of Vermont is known for its biology and life sciences programs.

Cancelled 1906, $4-6

A newer view of the Medical College.

Circa 1907, $4-6

The Billings Library is listed on the National Register of Historic Places and is a grand display of architecture. Designed in 1885 by Henry H. Richardson, the library is now the Billings Student Center (named after Frederick Billings—a native Vermont citizen).

Circa early 1900s, $4-6

Built during the years 1904-1907, Morrill Hall was to be the home of the Agriculture Department and the Agricultural Experiment Station. The building's namesake, U. S. Senator Justin Smith Morrill of Straffort, Vermont, was respsonsible for the 1862 Morrill Land Grant College Act. This legislation provided federal aid for public universities and land grant colleges.

Circa 1907, $4-6

Hospitals

Hospitals played a vital roll for the people of Burlington, whether considering the importance of the Mary Fletcher Hospital, the Post Hospital for Fort Ethan Allen, or one of the other facilities shown here through vintage preservation. Some of the hospitals available were community-based, while others supported military populations, educational medical venues, or other resources and options for Burlington's progressive healthcare system through the years. Pictured here are the Mary Fletcher Hospital, Fanny Allen Hospital, The Bishop De Goesbriand Hospital, the Post Hospital at Fort Ethan Allen, and the Lakeview Sanatorium.

Named after a Burlington resident, Mary Martha Fletcher, the hospital is supposedly the city's first public and largest hospital built in northern New England.

Cancelled 1906, $4-6

The Mary Fletcher Hospital is a teaching center for the University of Vermont.

Circa 1930s, $4-6

The Mary Fletcher Hospital, with a 310-bed capacity, also operates its own accredited School of Nursing.

Circa early 1900s, $4-6

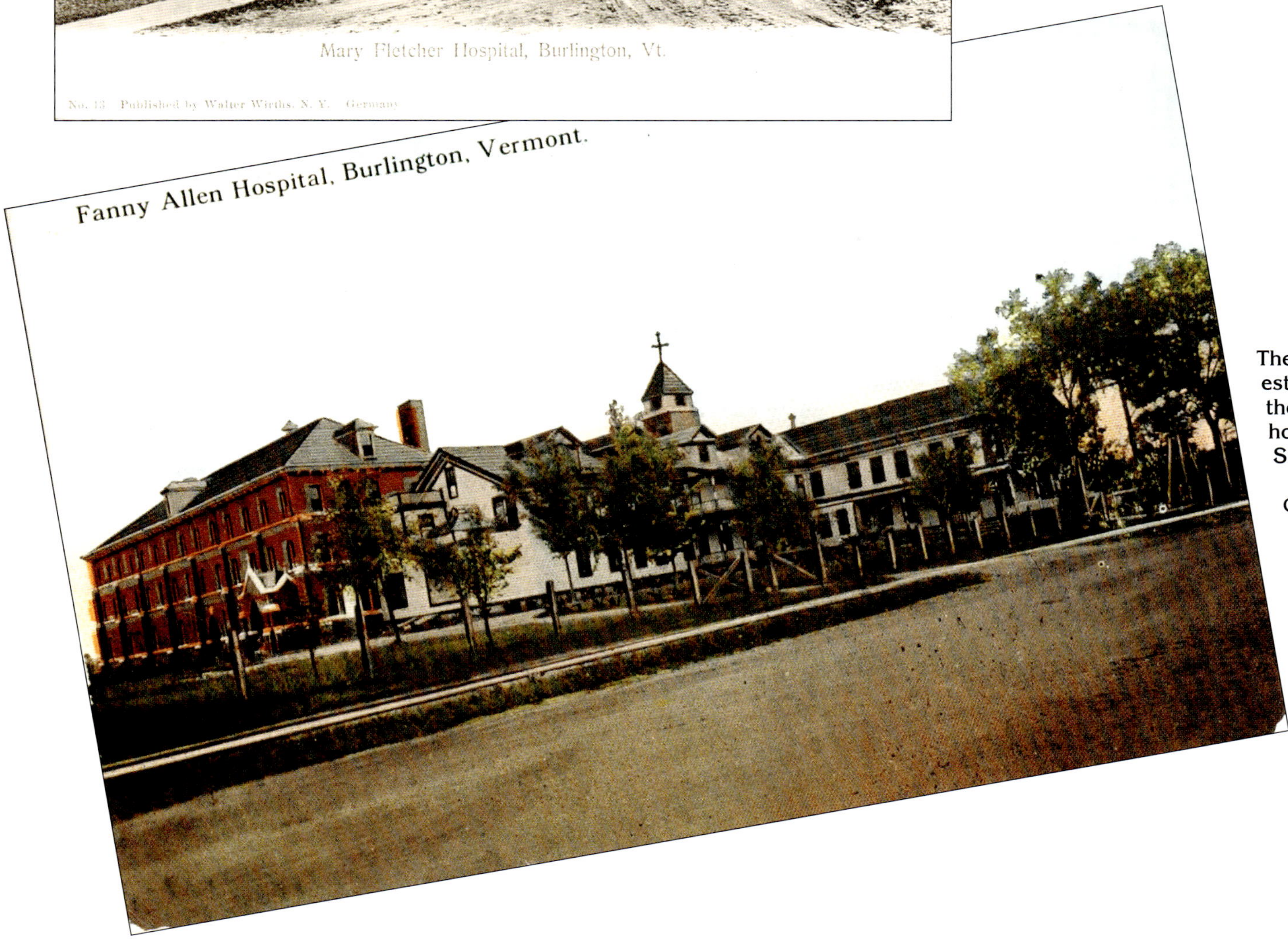

The Fanny Allen Hospital was established in 1894. Named after the daughter of Ethan Allen, the hospital was founded by the Sisters of St. Joseph.

Circa 1907, $4-6

The Fanny Allen Hospital merged with the Medical Center Hospital of Vermont in 1995 becoming part of the organization now called Fletcher Allen Healthcare. It is now referred to as the Fanny Allen Campus.

Circa 1907, $4-6

The Bishop De Goesbriand Hospital was built in 1924 in the memory of the first bishop of Vermont.

Circa 1914, $4-6

The hospital's namesake, De Goesbriand, became bishop in 1853 in Burlington. Bishop De Goesbriand was the son of a French nobleman.

Circa 1930s, $3-5

Built in 1894, the Base Hospital at Fort Ethan Allen was, at that time, in a period of its greatest growth. It is said that the current hospital is haunted by two soldiers who had burned to death in the nursing home located there.

Circa early 1900s, $4-6

The Lakeview Sanatorium in Burlington, this view from the Avenue looking at the Main Building. On this particular card, there is a small view of the rear of the building on the reverse.

Cancelled 1917, $5-7

Government & Public Buildings

From the first postal route in Vermont (1781) to the first town meeting (1787), Burlington has had a strong presence of government and historic values that continues today. Pictured here, you will see rare views of heritage displayed in lovely postcard images of City Hall, the Post Office, Weather Bureau, Public Library, Fort Ethan Allen, and others.

A view of City Hall. Burlington was chartered in 1763, but settlement did not begin until the 1770s. This was when the Allen brothers (Ethan and Ira) built a fort at Winooski River.

Cancelled 1950, $4-6

In 1787, the first town meeting was held, and the University of Vermont was recognized in 1791. City Hall Park came soon after the town common was set aside as public land.

Cancelled 1947, $4-6

The Post Office and Custom House. In 1910, this building was erected and housed offices for the Federal Court, U. S. States Attorney, and the Internal Revenue Service.

Circa 1907, $4-6

The Post Office and Custom House was dedicated to the memory of Charles P. Smith, III and Bailey H. Goldberg (both servicemen who lost their lives in battle).

Cancelled 1923, $4-6

The U. S. Weather Bureau, located on Main Street, was purchased by the University of Vermont and has since been home to the Pringle Herbarium, the Military Science Department, and the offices for the Department of Natural Resources.

Cancelled 1909, $4-6

The Mary Fletcher-Carnegie Library. In 1873, Mary L. Fletcher and her daughter (Mary M. Fletcher) donated $20,000 to the city for the Fletcher Free Library, with the funding designated to be spent half on books, half for an endowment for the library.

Circa 1907, $4-6

Later, in 1901, when the library outgrew it's location (in the Old City Hall), Andrew Carnegie donated an additional $50,000 to construct a new library. This new library opened in 1904.

Circa early 1900s, $4-6

Memorial Auditorium, located on the corner of North Union and Main Streets has always provided a wide range of entertainment for the residents of Burlington.

Circa 1930s, $3-5

The Ethan Allen Monument. Erected in 1873 at the burial place of the Revoluntionary war hereo. Ethan Allen, the eight-foot statue can be seen at the Green Mount Cemetery at the top of a hill overlooking Winooski.

Circa 1907, $3-5

Fort Ethan Allen looking from the Water Tower in Burlington, Vermont. The actual fort is located in Colchester and was named after Revolutionary War hero Ethan Allen.

Circa 1907, $5-7

The Fort Ethan Allen Water Tower was previously a stone water storage tower.

Circa 1914, $3-5

The Barracks at Fort Ethan Allen. Most of the military housing at the fort has been restored for use as housing for students and others.

Circa early 1900s, $5-7

The Artillery Barracks at Fort Ethan Allen. The fort has been an active military fort since 1894. In 1961, it was decommissioned.

Circa 1930s, $3-5

The Officers' Quarters at Fort Ethan Allen. Fort Ethan Allen is recognized as a national historic district.

Circa early 1900s, $3-5

Officers' Row at Fort Ethan Allen.

Cancelled 1915, $3-5

U. S. O. Club—the United Service Organization. This club provided Burlington soldiers entertainment during their off-duty hours.

Circa 1930s, $4-6

Parks

The parks of Burlington provide both recreational pursuits for visitors interested in boating, scenic views, or lush landscapes, and also significant educational tours of history through the times of the Revolution and the War of 1812. Spectacular scenery with rolling landscapes and abundant forestry are intermingled with slice of life historic remembrances of heroes from long ago. Tour Burlington's Ethan Allen Park, Battery Park, City Hall Park, and Queen City Park on the following pages.

The entrance to Ethan Allen Park. The sixty-seven-acre park opened in 1905, offering lovely views of the Green Mountains, Lake Champlain, and the Adirondacks. This is a historic park.

Cancelled 1920, $2-4

Another view of the entranceway to the Ethan Allen Park. Today, recreational activities abound at the park—rock climbing, hiking, biking.

Cancelled 1911, $1-3

The Ethan Allen Tower in the park. The Tower is situated on Indian Rock, the ancient lookout for the Indians. (Samuel de Champlain visited the tower in 1609.)

Cancelled 1908, $1-3

The Ethan Allen Tower and plaque in the park. The memorial plaque to Ethan Allen at the Tower was dedicated by the Daughters of the Revolutionary, the Green Mountain Chapter.

Cancelled 1911, $1-3

Split Rock Road, a lovely scenic area found within the Ethan Allen Park.

Circa 1914, $1-3

Four winding paths were created for their scenic beauty and wildlife in 1905—The Pinnacle, Table Rock Drive, River Bank Drive, and Eastern Drive.

Circa early 1900s, $1-3

Another view of the Pinnacle of Ethan Allen Park. This pinnacle was a lookout for two centuries. Settlers, looking for Indians and other enemies along the Lake Champlain and Winooski River, found this spot invaluable.

Cancelled 1910, $1-3

The entrance to Battery Park in Burlington. The artillery located at this park during the War of 1812 was the reason for its name.

Circa early 1900s, $1-3

The plaque at the entrance of Battery Park says "The Battery of thirteen guns on the ground repulsed an attack of three British gunboats, June 18, 1813. It was the defense of Burlington, and of the United States Army here encamped during the War of 1812. This tablet was erected by the Green Mountains Chapter, Daughters of the American Revolution, 1898."

Circa 1907, $2-4

During the War of 1812, American gunners defended the Park against the British. The historic battle is remembered by a single cannon.

Circa 1907, $2-4

In 1972, a Battery Park extension was added to the south end of the park.

Circa 1907, $2-4

Among the monuments in Battery Park, stands an eight-foot bronze statue of Civil War General William W. Wells, who was recognized as an excellent soldier.

Circa 1907, $1-3

A daytime scene from Battery Park looking out onto Lake Champlain.
Circa 1914, $1-3

Battery Park has some of the most scenic views in all of Vermont—here, a sunset on Lake Champlain.

Circa 1907, $1-3

Another view of a magnificent sunset from Battery Park.

Circa 1907, $3-5

The Burlington Water Front from Battery Park.

Circa 1907, $3-5

City Hall Park, named for its proximaty to the Colonial Revival-style City Hall, is a popular park located in the heart of the downtown area. Originally, in the 1790s, the park land was set aside for a courthouse, and now, situated around the property, are public and commercial buildings—even the old Ethan Allen Firehouse.

Cancelled 1927, $4-6

A view of the Soldiers' Monument, erected in 1907 in memory of fallen heros.

Circa 1914, $4-6

The City Hall Park, was known at one time as Court-House Square. To the right on the postcard sits City Hall with the United States flag raised high.

Circa early 1900s, $4-6

The lovely City Hall Park fountain. This fountain was recently replaced for a more modern fountain.

Circa early 1900s, $3-5

City Hall Park, Burlington, Vermont

City Hall Park with a very good view of the business community on the other side of the Park. The park consisted of two and one half acres of land and was situated by Church, Main, College, and St. Paul Streets.

Circa 1908, $4-6

Queen City Park is located on Queen City Park Road and Central Avenue.

Cancelled 1914, $3-5

An older time, showing the entrance to Queen City Park.

Circa early 1900s, $3-5

The trolley station at the entrance to Queen City Park. A picnic area is located to the right.

Cancelled 1912, $3-5

A lovely lake view in Queen City Park.

Cancelled 1912, $2-4

A beach scene at Queen City Park. The park had summer homes hidden in the green of the trees and along the lake shore.

Circa 1914, $2-4

Romantic Lovers Lane at Queen City Park.

Cancelled 1908, $2-4

Streets

Burlington's busy business district, aptly called the Church Street Central Business District, is located in the heart of the downtown area. Lined with opportunities for visitors—then and now—to conduct business or seek entertaining ways to pass time, this was a grand starting point. Shopping, lounging in a park, or frequenting the restaurants and hotels of the day were pastimes available to travelers or residents. In contrast, you will also see Burlington streets that are primarily residential, depicting the historic architectural designs of the turn-of-the-century.

Church Street in Burlington goes through the center of the Central Business District and downtown Burlington.

Cancelled 1910, $8-10

The area along Bridge Street between Main and Pearl Streets still retains much of its initial charm today, though there has been some new development in the north eastern section.

Circa 1930, $7-9

The intersection at Church and Main Streets shows sidewalks lined with stores and other commercial entities. Notice the interesting street sign in the middle of the intersection.

Circa 1907, $10-12

Church Street looking North from Bank Street. On the corner of church you will see a storefront advertising R. B. Stearns & Co. Mr. Stearns provided pharmacy services at varied locations in the downtown area until he died in 1902. Still, though the pharmacy changed hands more than once after his death, it stayed open in the community until 1958.

Circa 1914, $9-11

Church Street looking south. Notice the F. W. Woolworth store on the corner, a popular retail establishment that found success by putting slow-moving merchandise out for customers at the purchase price of five cents—thus the beginning of the 5 & 10 Cent Stores.

Circa 1914, $8-10

Church Street looking North from College Street.

Cancelled 1907, $9-11

Main Street, looking east from the Hotel Vermont.

Circa 1914, $8-10

A view along St. Paul Street with the City Hall Park bordering one side of the street.

Cancelled 1909, $7-9

St. Paul Street, looking north.

Cancelled 1912, $7-9

The corner of Main and St. Paul Streets.

Circa 1914, $7-9

South Prospect Street, looking north, and the beautiful grounds of the University of Vermont campus.

Circa 1907, $5-7

A picturesque view along South Winooski Avenue, looking south.
Cancelled 1912, $4-6

A tree-lined street in a lovely residential section of Burlington.
Cancelled 1945, $3-5

By Land and By Water

Though the War of 1812 had some bearing on Burlington, beyond having an army post and military hospital, it did not have as much of an impact as it had on other Vermont areas. Burlington was, however, becoming an important city—by land and by water. In fact, Burlington was establishing itself as a leading port for the nation, especially for importing lumber from Canada (only about forty miles north).

A continuous water passageway, the Lake Champlain Canal was completed in 1823, allowing transport for manufacturing and farming products, as well as lumber, between New York and Montreal and also within the state of Vermont. In the 1830s, Burlington became a accepted location for key industrial and business exchanges with Canada.

The Lake Champlain waterways were not the only form of transportation reaching out beyond the city's limits as the years rolled forward. Railroads (beginning with the completion of the Burlington Railroad to Rutland in 1849) assisted with lumber commerce transport, and then bolstered business in 1862 as farmers began to make headway in the dairy markets, transporting to other areas in New England and Canada.

As you will see in many of the hand-tinted early photography, streetcars also became important to Burlington's travelers. The first streetcar service in the city, the Winooski and Burlington Horse Railroad Company began in 1885. The era of streetcars ended for Burlington in 1929 as the newer trolleys came to town.

Regardless of transportation modes, one thing is clear as you step into these rare views of Burlington's past. The charm of this city can be shared by both land and by water.

A scenic view of land and water looking west from the Ethan Allen Tower. The Tower is a popular place for visitors to enjoy the nature of Burlington.

Circa 1907, $4-6

The Union Depot. Notice the arched covering of the building over the locomotive. Tracks entered and exited through arched doorways. As locomotives grew in size though, the iron doorways became problematic.

Circa 1907, $11-13

UNION STATION, BURLINGTON, VT.

The Union Station opened in 1916.

Cancelled 1920, $11-13

INTERIOR, UNION STATION, BURLINGTON, VT.

A view of the interior of the Union Station.

Circa 1914, $10-12

The waterways were the primary mode of transportation prior to the development of the rails. By 1809, the steamboat Vermont was operating on Lake Champlain.

Cancelled 1908, $9-11

Steamer Ticonderoga leaving Burlington. First launched in 1906, the Ticonderoga now resides on museum grounds as a hands-on exhibit at the Shelburne Museum.

Circa 1914, $9-11

The Ticonderoga was in service for thirty years, but was unable to compete with the increasingly popular automobile. Still, for a time, this steamer was queen of the era.

Cancelled 1910, $10-12

The Adirondacks and Lake Champlain from the shores of Burlington. The Adirondack Mountains, with their thousands of square miles of wilderness, are the perfect backdrop for Lake Champlain's spectacular waterfronts.

Circa 1914, $6-8

A Lake Champlain view of a steamer in the foreground and the Adirondacks on far shores. The 120-mile-long and 12-mile-wide (at the widest point) lake flows north to the St. Lawrence River.

Circa 1914, $4-6

A moonlight scene on Lake Champlain, with sparkling lights dancing on calm waters.

Cancelled 1912, $2-4

A visitor to Lake Champlain in Burlington in 1910 wrote in her message, "This is the most beautiful city I have ever been in."

Cancelled 1910, $2-4

Lake Champlain and Juniper Island. The Island and the lighthouse on the island are privately owned.

Circa 1907, $1-3

A view from along the beautiful water front of Lake Champlain with its stunning views of the mountains. The Lake is as much as 300-400 feet deep in some places, but averages about 65 feet in depth.

Circa 1907, $3-5

A view looking at Burlington from Lake Champlain. There are lovely historic communities close to its shoreline.

Circa 1907, $4-6

The Harbor is located at the central area for Lake Champlain and at the widest of the lake.

Circa 1907, $3-5

Another view of the Harbor in Burlington. The Harbor area is now noted for great fishing during the Spring through the late Summertime, and is said to offer the greatest variety of freshwater fish in the Northeast.

Cancelled 1907, $5-7

The two towns, Milton and South Hero, Vermont are connected by the Sand Bar Bridge that crosses Lake Champlain near Burlington.

Circa 1914, $3-5

A dock scene on Lake Champlain. Even today one can see sailboats lining the forty marinas.

Circa 1907, $4-6

The New Streamline Ferry and Pier. Bridges across wide lakes were thought to be impractical, therefore, ferries have been a viable solution to crossing Lake Champlain.

Circa 1930s, $5-7

There were ferries for both automobiles and passengers. It was even found that ferries were well-suited for horse transport. The earliest documented horse-boat on Lake Champlain was in 1826. This scene shows ferry service running between Burlington and Port Kent, New York on Lake Champlain.

Circa 1930s, $4-6

Chace Mills—a 90,000 square-foot energy facility—has been upgraded for energy efficiency, but its charm and historic character still remain.

Circa 1907, $4-6

Because the harbor at Burlington had little protection from winds coming from the south and northwest, a federally funded breakwater began in 1837. In 1857, wooden lighthouses were placed at the ends of the breakwater, as seen here, to mark entrances to the harbor.

Circa 1907, $7-9

Eventually, the wooden lighthouses were replaced with steel towers (circa 1925 and 1950). Less weather damage occurred because of the replacement, but some of the lighthouse magic was lost.

Circa 1914, $6-8

The Lake Champlain Yacht Club was founded in 1887 and built at the end of College Street.

Circa 1907, $5-7

The Lake Champlain Yacht Club was the fifty-fourth yacht club to be founded in the nineteenth century.

Cancelled 1909, $5-7

A waterfront yacht club slip in Burlington. In the early 1900s, boathouses lined the waterfront.

Cancelled 1907, $4-6

A municipal bathing beach on Lake Champlain. There are 587 miles of shoreline along the lake.

Cancelled 1936, $3-5

The beautiful Crescent Beach. Beaches along Lake Champlain sometimes included old and grand trees as shown here.

Cancelled 1910, $2-4

Red Rocks Park, in Southern Burlington, is situated on 100 acres on Shelburne Bay. The area is mostly woodland, but also has shoreline for beaches.

Circa early 1900s, $2-4

Red Rocks, Burlington, Vermont.

A view of the wooded area along an approach to Lake Champlain.

Cancelled 1910, $1-3

A view looking across Lake Champlain from Red Rocks.

Cancelled 1903, $2-4

Two visitors at Red Rocks enjoy the area called, Shelving Rocks, in one wooded retreat.

Circa 1907, $2-4

A shady drive near Burlington at Shelburne Farms—the establishment created as a model of an agricultural estate in 1886 by William Seward and Lila Vanderbilt Webb.

Circa 1907, $1-3

Shelburne Farms at the sea wall and Lake Champlain.

Circa 1907, $2-4

Property totalling 130 acres of lush trees, vegetation, cliffs, beaches, and other natural wonders can be seen (then and now) at Rock Point. Rock Point was deeded to the Episcopal Diocese of Vermont since 1854 to be used as a home for future Bishops and educational pursuits.

Cancelled 1914, $3-5

In the nineteenth century, Burlington Bay (located at the widest area of Lake Champlain) was a hub of commerce for the area. Steamboat traffic and ferries were common sights.

Cancelled 1904, $4-6

Sunset Rock at Rock Point in Burlington. Aptly named because of the enchanting sunsets that can be seen from the overlook, Sunset Rock continues to be a popular recreational area long Lake Champlain.

Cancelled 1930, $1-3

A glimpse of Malletts Bay (just north of Burlington) from the Lake Champlain Club at Marble Island.

Cancelled 1933, $1-3

A tributary of Lake Champlain, the winding Winooski River is approximately ninety miles long. It is one of the state's most significant rivers because it forms a major valley way from the Lake through the Green Mountains. The city, Winooski, is situated along the river approximately five miles upstream from its mouth on the eastern edge of Burlington.

Circa 1914, $1-3

In the nineteenth century, the Winooski River was integral to the logging industry and was used for transportation of timber.

Circa 1907, $1-3

The word, Winooski (the river and the city), is taken from the Indian word, Winoskitegw, meaning onion land river.

Cancelled 1907, $3-5

Another view of the Winooski Falls with it's churning water.

Circa 1907, $4-6

The lovely image of historic, High Bridge bridge, in Winooski, portrays a stark contrast between nature and man.

Cancelled 1908, $3-5

The Gorge in Winooski, near Burlington.

Cancelled 1939, $3-5

The Winooski Valley, showing the winding Winooski River and Mount Mansfield in the distance. A primary reason for Ira Allen settling in the area was the waterpower from the lower falls of the Winooski River. This power was needed for the mills that manufactured textiles and other products.

Circa 1914, $2-4

Snow-capped Mount Mansfield, Camel Hump, and Mount Range can be seen in the distance of this landscape. From the eastside, Mount Mansfield has been said by some to resemble a face.

Cancelled 1912, $3-5

At an elevation of 4,083 feet, Camel's Hump (which is just to the south of Mount Mansfield) is the highest undeveloped mountain in Vermont. Mount Mansfield holds the record as the highest mountain in Vermont.

Circa 1914, $3-5

A view of lovely Eagle Bay.

Circa early 1900s, $2-4

Another view of Mount Mansfield from the University Tower. The Converse Dormitory is seen in the foreground.

Circa 1914, $3-5

More Faces of Burlington!

Take a look at more of the random faces of Burlington—a little more of everything! Buildings and parks to landscapes and sunsets. Harbors and lakes to hotels and busy streets! It's all here for you in Burlington!

The U. S. Post Office and Court House.

Circa 1930s, $4-6

The current City Hall building has been recognized by the Environmental Protection Agency as one of the top energy-performance buildings in 2002.

Circa early 1900s, $3-5

The Municipal Auditorium (also known as the Memorial Auditorium) is located near the Edmunds Middle School at the corner of North Union and Main Streets.

Circa 1914, $4-6

The Mary Fletcher-Carnegie Library (also known as the Carnegie Libary as shown here). Andrew Carnegie was convinced that having access to books was a means to positive changes in the lives of people. Thus, he became such a benefactor for libraries around the country.

A folk hero of Burlington and beyond, Ethan Allen (1738-1789) was a farmer who became a statesman.

Circa 1914, $2-4

An important medical facility in Burlington's past, The Bishop De Goesbriand Hospital, in the early seventies, was replaced by ten different medical practices that had gathered together to become the University Health Center. This new establishment was placed on the site of the former hospital.

Cancelled 1905, $3-5

This hospital was named for Burlington resident Mary Martha Fletcher. The hospital is reported to be Burlington's first and largest hospital.

Cancelled 1905, $2-4

Another view of the Ethan Allen Club, noted as a most aristocratic club.

Circa 1930s, $3-5

The Ira Allen Chapel at the University of Vermont is listed on the National Register of Historic Places.

Circa 1907, $2-4

THE CAMPUS. UNIVERSITY OF VERMONT, BURLINGTON.

A view of the campus at the University of Vermont.

Circa 1914, $2-4

College of Medicine, University of Vermont at Burlington (Photo by Jary) 167

A photographic view of the College of Medicine at the University of Vermont.

Circa 1914, $3-5

Main Campus, University of Vermont, Burlington, Vt. © 53 Vermont Press 169

A birds-eye view of the University of Vermont campus.

Cancelled 1955, $3-5

The Billings Library. Frederick Billings (the library's namesake) was not only the President of the Northern Pacific Railroad, but also the person after which Billings, Montanna, was named.

Circa 1914, $3-5

American gunners, with help from the President, defended Battery Park successfully against a British attack on August 13, 1813.

Circa 1907, $2-4

In 1870, the City of Burlington was deeded the park land of Battery Park.

Cancelled 1906, $2-4

A calming view of Battery Park.

Cancelled 1906, $1-3

The Lafayette Statue is a reminder to students of Lafayette's love for his country.

Circa 1930s, $2-4

Another view of the Lafayette Statute on the University Green.

Circa 1907, $2-4

The Ethan Allen Memorial Tower located at Indian Rock affords an unrivaled view of the Adirondacks, Lake Champlain, and the Green Mountains.

Circa 1907, $2-4

A lush walkway on Lovers' Lane in Queen City Park.

Cancelled 1910, $1-3

Visitors lounge in the Queen City Park.

Circa 1907, $1-3

A peaceful scene along the beach at Queen City Park.

Circa 1907, $2-4

Another view of St. Mary's Cathedral, in Burlington.

Circa 1907, $4-6

The Van Ness House boasted of having ice made on the premises.

Cancelled 1910, $4-6

The Allenwood Inn had a lovely Japanese Tea Garden on the property, for guests to enjoy.

Circa 1914, $1-3

The Allenwood's Sunken Garden.

Circa 1930s, $1-3

A lovely water garden at the Allenwood Inn.

Circa 1930s, $1-3

This lovely scene could be found on the property of the Allenwood Inn. The Inn, in addition to lush gardens and wooded havens, was (when this postcard was printed) also home to the Lake Champlain Yacht Club.

Cancelled 1936, $1-3

A busy harbor scene.

Cancelled 1933, $4-6

Sailing vessels on the calm, lake-front waters.

Cancelled 1909, $3-5

A park-like scene at Shelburne Farms by the Sea Wall and Lake Champlain (North, near Burlington).

Cancelled 1910, $1-3

Looking out onto the harbor.

Circa 1907, $4-6

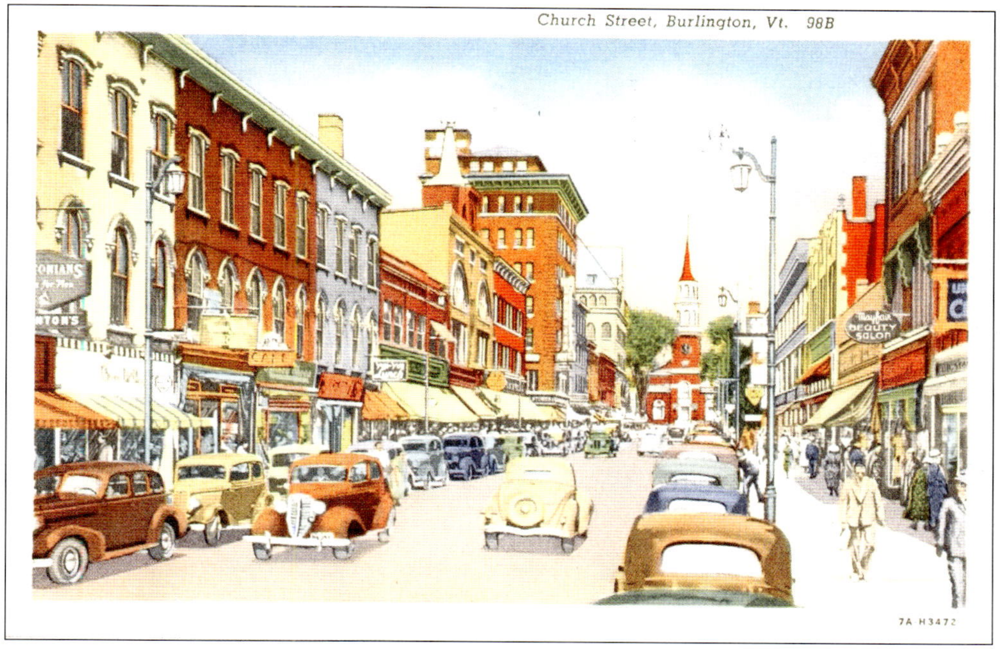

A view of Church Street. Note the Mayfair Beauty Salon on the right and Thom McCann shoes on the left.

Cancelled 1940, $7-9

Lower Church Street. Notice the City Hall Grill on the right side of the street.

Circa 1930s, $6-8

Church Street looking North to the Unitarian Church. The American Legion Post is situated on the right side of the street. The American Legion is a community-service organization that was chartered by Congress in 1919 as a veterans organization.

Circa 1920s, $6-8

Yachting, a popular water activity, on Lake Champlain.

Circa 1907, $2-4

Eagle Bay on Lake Champlain.

Circa 1907, $2-4

Recreational swimming on a municipal beach on Lake Champlain.

Cancelled 1929, $2-4

Mount Mansfield from Burlington, Vermont. Today, the mountain is a popular hiking attraction.

Circa 1907, $2-4

A scenic view of the High Bridge at the Winooski Gorge.

Circa 1914, $1-3

The beautiful Winooski River, with water reflecting like glass, near the High Bridge.

Circa 1914, $1-3

An interesting depiction of Shelburne Bay by moonlight.

Circa early 1900s, $1-3

The Winooski River Gorge, near Burlington.

Circa 1907, $1-3

Old Wood Road, in Red Rocks—
a lavish landscape.

Circa 1930s, $1-3

The Winooski Falls in Burlington.

Circa 1907, $1-3

Moonlight on Lake Champlain, a sparkling
view that is matched by none.

Circa 1907, $1-3

Bibliography & Resources

AAA Tour Book. "Burlington." Heathrow, FL: AAA Publishing, 2001.

American Co-Masonry, American Federation of Human Rights. "Introduction to Freemasonry." http://www.co-masonry.org/

Answers.com. "Vermont." http://www.answers.com/topic/vermont—check

Branch Out Burlington. "The Trees at Rock Point." http://www.branchoutburlington.org/events/treewalk/rockpointtreewalk.pdf

The Burlington Free Press. "Ticonderoga marks 100th anniversary." Thursday, July 13, 2006. http://www.burlingtonfreepress.com/apps/pbcs.dll/article?AID=/20060708/OPINION/607080318/1006&theme=

The Burlington School District. http://www.bsdvt.org/schools/edmundsmid/history.htm

Champlain Shores in the Adirondacks Lake. http://www.goadirondack.com/

College Street Congregational Church. "A Brief Edition of an Extraordinary History." http://www.collegestreetchurchvt.org/history.html

Diocese of Burlington, Vermont. A Commemorative of The Solemn Liturgy of Dedication of the Cathedral Church of the Immaculate Conception. Vermont: Diocese of Burlington, Vermont, 1977.

Directory of Burlington Vermont Area Web Sites and Information. "Society and Culture, Christianity and Religion." http://burlingtonvt.org/society-and-culture/christianity-and-religion/more.html

The Encyclopedia Britannica. "Trinity College." http://www.britannica.com/ebi/article-9341271

The Howard Center for Human Services. "Howard Center's 130 Year History." http://www.howardcenter.org. Fall 2003

Lake Champlain Yacht Club. "North American Yacht Clubs, Power Squadrons & Sailing Clubs Founded in the 19th Century." http://www.lcyc-vt.org/About_the_Club/history.htm#lcyc2

Lighthouse Friends. "Burlington Breakwater North, VT." http://www.lighthousefriends.com/light.asp?ID=873

Lindauer Simmon, Virginia. "Vermont's Other Playground." Vermont Guide. http://www.vermontguides.com/2006/04-apr/lake.html

Institute of Nautical Archaeology. "Hoofbeats Over the Water: I. N. A. Research on Horse-Powered Ferryboats. http://ina.tamu.edu/LChorseferry.htm.

Onion City. "City of Winooski, VT; City Name." http://www.onioncity.com

St. Michael's College. Historic Fort Ethan Allen: The Hospital; http://personalweb.smcvt.edu/thefort/buildings/Hospital.htm

The University of Vermont. "Ira Allen Chapel." http://www.uvm.edu/~campus/iraallen/iraallenhistory.html

World Book Encyclopedia. "Vermont, The Green Mountain State." Chicago: Field Enterprises, Inc., 1949.

BILLINGS LIBRARY, BURLINGTON, VT.